ATHENA

APEX

BY CHRISTINE HA

WWW.APEXEDITIONS.COM

Apex is distributed by North Star Editions:
sales@northstareditions.com | 888-417-0195

Produced for Apex by Red Line Editorial.

Photographs ©: Shutterstock Images, cover, 1, 4–5, 8, 9, 10–11, 16–17, 18–19, 20–21, 22–23, 24, 25, 26–27; iStockphoto, 6–7, 12–13, 14–15, 29

Library of Congress Control Number: 2020952908

ISBN
978-1-63738-013-0 (hardcover)
978-1-63738-049-9 (paperback)
978-1-63738-119-9 (ebook pdf)
978-1-63738-085-7 (hosted ebook)

Printed in the United States of America
Mankato, MN
082021

NOTE TO PARENTS AND EDUCATORS

Apex books are designed to build literacy skills in striving readers. Exciting, high-interest content attracts and holds readers' attention. The text is carefully leveled to allow students to achieve success quickly. Additional features, such as bolded glossary words for difficult terms, help build comprehension.

TABLE OF CONTENTS

CHAPTER 1

SAVED FROM DANGER

A hero and his crew were in danger. Their boat sailed toward two huge rocks. The rocks crashed together without warning.

Many myths tell of heroes making long, dangerous journeys.

Athena helped many heroes with their quests.

Odysseus sailed home to Ithaca. A statue of him stands on this island.

HEADING HOME

Odysseus was one of Athena's favorite heroes. She helped him make a long journey home. She showed him what to do. And she guarded him from attacks.

CHAPTER 2

WAR AND WISDOM

Athena was the goddess of war and wisdom. She was the daughter of Zeus. Her birth was unusual. She sprang from his forehead. And she was fully grown and wearing armor.

Athena was Zeus's oldest child and favorite daughter.

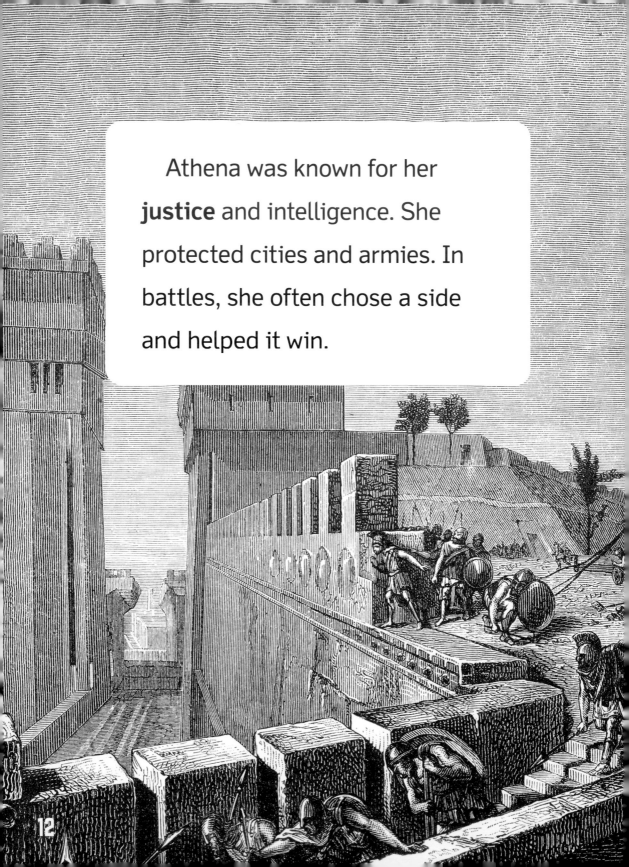

Athena was known for her **justice** and intelligence. She protected cities and armies. In battles, she often chose a side and helped it win.

Athena helped armies make plans to win battles. For example, she helped the Greeks make the Trojan Horse.

Athena helped the Greeks win the Trojan War. They hid inside a huge horse to invade the city of Troy.

Athena was also a goddess of crafts. She was skilled at **spinning** and **weaving**.

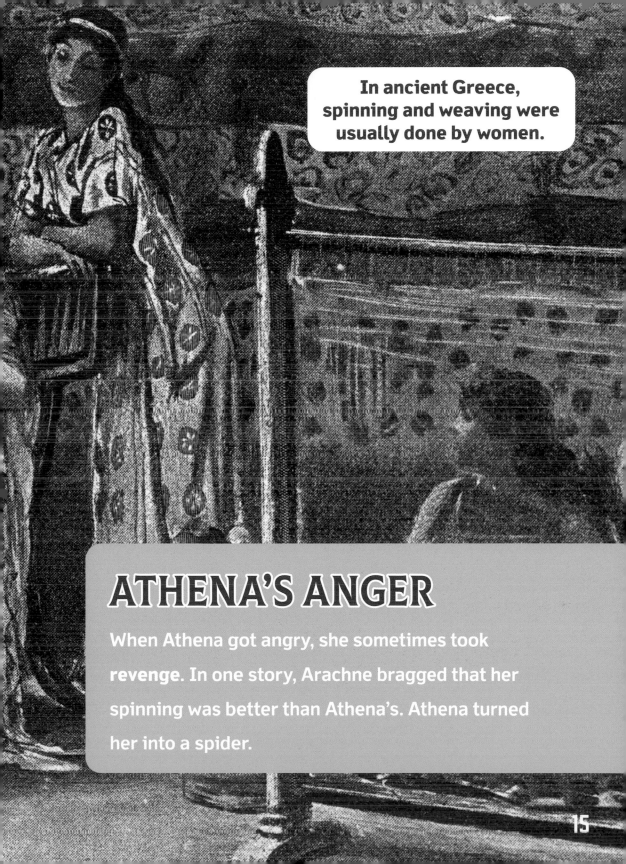

In ancient Greece, spinning and weaving were usually done by women.

ATHENA'S ANGER

When Athena got angry, she sometimes took **revenge**. In one story, Arachne bragged that her spinning was better than Athena's. Athena turned her into a spider.

CHAPTER 3

HELPING HEROES

Athena could be **stern**. But she liked people who were brave. She helped and protected them.

Athena often gave heroes gifts or helped them fight.

For example, she helped Perseus defeat Medusa. Medusa could turn people to stone with one look.

Medusa was a monster with snakes for hair.

OTHER ADVENTURES

Athena gave Bellerophon a golden **bridle**. He used it to tame the winged horse Pegasus. Athena gave Hercules a golden sword. He used it to kill a monster.

The Greeks believed Athena invented many useful things. These items included ships, chariots, rakes, and plows.

In some myths, Athena's shield had Medusa's face on it. It could turn people to stone.

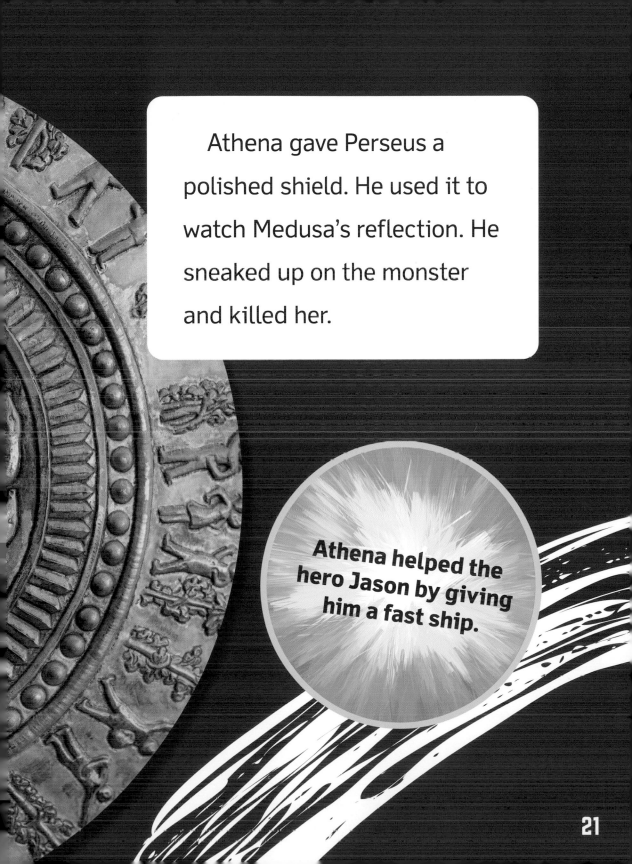

Athena gave Perseus a polished shield. He used it to watch Medusa's reflection. He sneaked up on the monster and killed her.

Athena helped the hero Jason by giving him a fast ship.

CHAPTER 4

ATHENA'S CITY

Athena was the **guardian** of Athens. She and Poseidon had both wanted this position. So, they had a contest. Each gave the city a gift.

Athena is sometimes shown holding an owl.

Poseidon made a **spring**. Athena planted an olive tree. The city's king picked Athena. He named the city after her.

Olive trees were valuable. They could provide food, oil, and wood.

Athens had pictures of Athena and her symbols on its coins.

ATHENA'S SYMBOLS

Owls and snakes were symbols of Athena. In Greece, owls represented wisdom. Snakes represented **cautiousness**. Olive leaves could be signs of Athena, too.

The Parthenon was a famous temple to Athena. It was built on a hill in the city of Athens.

The people of Athens built temples in Athena's honor. They also had a big festival each year. It included a parade, music, and sports.

One temple had a huge statue of Athena inside. She stood 38 feet (11.5 m) tall.

COMPREHENSION QUESTIONS

Write your answers on a separate piece of paper.

1. Write a few sentences explaining the main ideas of Chapter 2.

2. If you had been the ruler of Athens, would you have chosen Athena or Poseidon? Why?

3. What was one of Athena's skills?

   A. music
   B. weaving
   C. sports

4. Why might Athena sometimes be stern?

   A. Her sense of justice would make her enforce the rules.
   B. Her sense of pride would make her say rude things.
   C. Her fear of losing would make her act unwisely.

5. What does **crush** mean in this book?

*Athena saw the rocks begin to slam shut. Soon, they would **crush** the hero's boat.*

   A. break by pressing on
   B. stay away from
   C. hold very still

6. What does **invade** mean in this book?

*Athena helped the Greeks win the Trojan War. They hid inside a huge horse to **invade** the city of Troy.*

   A. attack and take over
   B. run away from
   C. give lots of money to

Answer key on page 32.

GLOSSARY

bridle
A set of straps that allow a person to control a horse.

cautiousness
Being careful and looking out for danger.

chariots
Two-wheeled carts pulled by horses or other animals.

guardian
A person who protects something or someone.

justice
Doing what is right and fair.

revenge
Getting back at someone who has caused hurt or anger.

spinning
Twisting material together to make a long thread.

spring
A place where water bubbles up from underground.

stern
Serious and firm, especially in making people follow the rules.

weaving
Making fabric by lacing threads or strips of material together.

TO LEARN MORE

BOOKS

Buckey, A. W. *Greek Gods, Heroes, and Mythology.*
  Minneapolis: Abdo Publishing, 2019.

Menzies, Jean. *Greek Myths: Meet the Heroes, Gods, and
  Monsters of Ancient Greece.* New York: DK Publishing,
  2020.

Temple, Teri. *Athena: Goddess of Wisdom, War, and Crafts.*
  Mankato, MN: The Child's World, 2019.

ONLINE RESOURCES

Visit **www.apexeditions.com** to find links and resources
related to this title.

ABOUT THE AUTHOR

Christine Ha lives in Minnesota. She enjoys reading
and learning about myths and legends from around the
world. Athens was one of her all-time favorite travel
destinations.

INDEX

Answer Key:
1. Answers will vary; **2.** Answers will vary; **3.** B; **4.** A; **5.** A; **6.** A